everyday
zen

everyday
zen

stephanie jt russell

ariel·books

**Andrews McMeel
Publishing**

Kansas City

Designed by Junie Lee Tait

ISBN: 0-7407-3351-6
02 03 04 05 06 BID 10 9 8 7 6 5 4 3 2 1

Library of Congress Catalog Card Number:
2002111565

For Pete, plain as summer rain

contents

beginning like
beginning

At this moment what is there that you
  lack?
Nirvana presents itself before you,
Where you stand is the Land of Purity.
Your person, the body of Buddha.

—Hakuin

As far in the past as the fifteenth century, when silk and spice traders brought Asian culture into the Western spotlight, Eastern religions have attracted both exotic fascination and serious study. Among all the spiritual practices that have emerged from Asia, Buddhism has likely made the biggest impact. And within it, Zen tradition seems to have gathered the widest appeal.

Zen teachings are embodied in a spare, direct manner that urges the practitioner to squarely face life as it is, not as she or he might wish it to be. Simple, unadorned, and immediate, Zen sensibility lends itself to a universal understanding of essential

Buddhist attitudes and concepts.

Basic Buddhism teaches that the physical, human world is impermanent. Therefore, attachment to material things leads only to yet more worldly attachment and increasingly diminished spiritual fulfillment. To transmit the essence of impermanence, Zen teachings accent the need to become fully present in the moment.

Zen mind sees daily life as the main vehicle for higher awareness. This principle urges that enlightenment is embedded in the essential acts of the day—rising, working, eating, even sleeping. Used intelligently, these things offer a passage to freedom from judgment, fear, and the cycle of expectation and disappointment.

Zen is a life saturated with simplicity and depth—in everything and in nothing. In the laundry room, the boardroom, and a room without walls: the human heart.

Busy Getting Nowhere

Self-justification is like pouring a
cup of sand into the ocean.

Either Way

Truth has no favorites. When the
heart speaks in silence, everything
listens. When the voice speaks for
the heart, it does not matter if
there's a listener or a speech.
Truth is there anyway.

Water Rising to Its Level

Halfhearted action makes mud of a
mountain stream. Walk into your
work with everything you have and
leave with yet more clarity.

Nowhere Else Matters

This sea without shores, this road
without a beginning! How good to
be here, where it's all happening
at once.

Inner Fire

Silence consumes itself like the
wick of an oil lamp. Subtle light
everywhere!

Perfectly Happy Alone

If someone calls your name, have
you found yourself yet?

Zen: nothing, nothing, nothing at all!

Wasting Time, Part One

Birth, death, sleeping in between:
Why not wake up to what you were
born for?

Hiding from Nothing

Harder and harder the storm
howls. Will you stay inside forever?

Deconstructing Babel

Religions are simply different
roads leading to the same point.
How many names for heaven exist?
None of them change the nature of
sky itself.

Dog Chasing Its Tail

Okay, keep arguing about the nature of life: That brings you no closer to understanding the nature of your *self*.

Dancing in Step

Forget preconceptions and
synchronize with reality. Then
your own rhythm will emerge in
the music of everyday life.

Getting the Point

Talking philosophy is fine for sake
parties. Realizing oneness is Zen.
There's no place like home to find
it—or at work, or in the street.

This thing, that thing—all that matters is nothing.

Putting Down Your Fists

Lose your point of view and find
the Self.

Changing Position

Small-minded, we stay in what we
know. When we recognize the
infinite cosmos in ourselves,
everything becomes new.

Getting Quiet

Agitation of mind scrambles the
language of life.

What Do We Know?

Ask questions, be puzzled, wet
your towel with tears. It's okay—
confusion and answers anticipate
each other, like dancers in motion
till the end of a song.

Who Leads the Shepherd?

The internal teacher is born within you and does not need to be seen. The external teacher shows up to remind you of the inward path.

Following a teacher?
Wear a blindfold—and open
inner sight.

35

Gorging on Ego

Sweet or bitter, honeyed or rancid,
we are drawn to taste it all. Eat, eat!
The Self looks on unconcerned,
content to observe the feast.

Zen Mind Defined

Getting free of the idea of
getting free.

seeing what's there

We're usually so busy trying to make things occur according to plan that we rarely see what's happening beneath the surface of events. What is it to really *see*, without the dense filters of our desires, expectations, and preconceptions?

To receive life with more subtle insight, a Zen practitioner strips away the excess mental tensions of urgent daily activity. At first, this isn't an easy thing to do. But the basics of Zen mind are lodged in simply paying attention to the moment. This implies quieting the mind. And that means being fully present, *now*—not thrashing around in an obsolete past or worrying about an unknown future.

The Zen maneuver is to catch ourselves straying from the moment and focus on what's real now. Take a breath . . . and *stay* with the breath. This relaxes the body, sharpens the mind, and fluidly connects each moment to the next.

Being truly present is a creative, vital approach to life. Above all, Zen mind *savors* the moment. Go ahead

and taste its flavor, smell its fra-
grance. Let it tell you what you're
experiencing. Do not let it leave
your sight.

Just There, in the Mirror

Can you look at yourself without analyzing? The real "you" is more than a collection of memories, experience, and ideas. You are changing every day, every hour. Let yourself grow wild as a cattail on the marshes.

Cosmic Perfection,
Part One

Human beings are always trying to
fix things. Our hardest lesson is
seeing perfection in the imperfect
nature of the world.

Conflict

Conflict is never what it appears
to be. Beneath the surface of
emotional reactions lies a chance to
transform the most bewildering
questions into the most
enlightened answers.

Transparent Reflection

Our imperfect nature is a mirror
of life itself. In seeing ourselves
clearly, we find ways to outgrow
destructive behaviors and ideas.
Old patterns shatter when we
transform our relationship to
familiar, basic things.

Wake up! You are here!

Missing Nothing

When you finally see that you're
not attentive, paying attention
will start becoming a priority.
Then there is no such thing as
wasted time.

Beyond the Senses

Beneath external noise and clatter,
each day radiates its teachings
in silence.

No Illusions

Seeking approval from others?
You might as well seek it in a
bloom or a bee. Like people, they
are simply there to be enjoyed.

One Little Universe

How often do you try to fill open
space with needless action or
words? Emptiness leaves room
for things to just be.

Sshhh! There's no improving on silence.

53

Wasting Time, Part Two

Wanting something that cannot be
had: the future, yesterday,
someone else's life. Stay here
and receive what is happening now:
a gift without end.

Neutral Witnessing

When you listen with open ears,
there's no confusion or conflict.
You are simply hearing another
sound, word, or idea. None of it
is permanent and all of it is a
teaching. Stay in the moment
and just listen.

Drive, eat, work—but do it awake!

Having Everything,
Needing Nothing

Zen mind says we already possess
what we need. Why bother desiring
more than what we have right now,
here in the moment?

One Room, One Chair

Feel the pleasure of sitting in a
finely wrought chair. How delight-
ful to pay attention to such an
object. It's like watching a single
maple leaf riding the wind.

Cosmic Perfection,
Part Two

Perfect and *imperfect* live together in nothingness. Think of Zen this way: Sometimes it rains and sometimes it doesn't. All that remains is acceptance.

being alive

In general society, the mechanics of doing leave little room for just being. It's easy to forget that life is more than a frantic series of tasks, goals, and accomplishments. This kind of intense action is not merely tiring and limiting. In terms of living a full, rich, spiritual life, it's also deeply impractical.

Still, spiritual life is often seen as a quaint sidebar to "real life." Zen mind turns this notion on its ear and asserts that life itself is not real without spiritual attention. That attention is grounded in all the things of daily existence—the concrete actions that show us how we're really living.

How do we relate to ourselves? To each other? Do our daily tasks become a reason to avoid awareness? And if so, why *not* use them to become more aware, more in tune, more alive?

Step into the moment and trust life. It wants us to know we are a part of its mystery, its question, and its truth.

Fullness

One cup of water contains the
whole spring.

Emptiness

A street lamp burning alone cares
nothing for its brilliance.

Here and Now

Snow on treetops: What could
be better?

Presence

A child with a ball knows exactly
where she is.

Self-Knowledge

Self-knowledge is like looking
through a window and gazing into
a mirror at the same time.

Underground Overflow

Zen is always inside you, waiting to
be used. Its water never dries up.
Even when you feel hurt, angry, or
depleted, you can instantly return
to the infinite river within. Make
the choice, flip the switch, and sit
in silence.

Walk Away the Trouble

Everyday problems can seem
unsolvable. They are not. Walk
around the block and take in the
world: the topiary, the trees, a
paper cup crumpled in the grass.
When you return home, your
solution will be inside the door.

Different Idea, Same Response, Part One

Someone says you're a good person: Smile. Someone says you're a bad person: Smile again.

Everything is silly.
Everything is serious. Don't choose.

The Permanent
Wake-Up Call

Use every situation to wake
up—your job, your leisure, your
supper. When you *want* to wake
up, nothing is an obstacle and
everything is a path
to consciousness.

Paradise Found

Surrender is learning and learning
is order. If powerful people lived
in a state of surrender, the world
would become an Eden.

Modest Wisdom

Zen mind is poured into all things.
It wears experience as humbly as a
comfortable old shoe.

Forget the past—drink some tea!

On Your Own, Part One

No authority can give you order,
peace, or understanding. Live
simply. Let the moment teach
everything you need. When you
stop craving exotic escape from
daily life, knowledge arises from
simple things you already know.

Seeking God?

Each path marks a river; each river flows into the same lake. Go anywhere—and the search is over. Go anywhere—and it begins again.

Where You Are Real

Savor solitude. When you know
you're part of the whole universe,
loneliness begets compassion
and creativity.

The Mountain Surrenders

What erodes jagged rock? The way
to penetrate all harshness and
severity: with soft water and
vacant wind.

Subsiding Ego

In the Zen mind, humility opens
the portal to understanding. Let
yourself be shaped by daily life, like
a stone awash in the riverbed.

Inspiration: Like a Breath

The highest art is unsophisticated.
It expresses a pure moment in time
that can never be duplicated.

Cosmic Perfection,
Part Three

Real knowledge never comes in the
ways we devise. Deep understanding defies logic. And everything we
learn is another step into the
unknown.

Confidence

Confidence is recognizing that
hindsight gives birth to foresight.

From Kitchen to Pavement

The most common parts of your day bear uncommon wisdom. Nothing in life is really predictable: It all depends on your approach.

Lightness of Heart

The seriousness of spiritual devel-
opment should be balanced with
humor and innocence. Zen mind
restores the lightness of heart we
felt as children. We can bring that
into everything—even our most
sober duties.

Sit apart from idiocy:
There is nothing to prove by fighting.

Intimacy

Intimacy is sharing a deep understanding in silence, or even at a
distance. Sometimes we feel most
deeply connected with others when
they are absent.

Tending the Fire

There is no excuse for boredom.
It's up to you to continually
rediscover your purpose. The
truly passionate soul is a master
of freshly rekindling the flame
of life every day.

Inspired Commitment

A quiet heart reflects the finest
gift a human being can present
to the world.

permanent
impermanence

The simple fact of change remains the hardest thing for people to understand and accept. Yet it's one of the few things we can rightly count on, day after day.

Even when we resist change, it inevitably causes us to question our part in life. And sometimes, we must work to catch up with changes that occur despite our resistance.

Zen mind not only accepts change, it *relishes* a robust, unexpected shake-up of the status quo. When the movement of life alters reality, it means that we have a chance to break out of stagnation and evolve to a higher level.

The fact is, we're constantly

changing. Beyond physical aging, our interior lives undergo thousands of shifts every day. Moods, emotions, intentions, and desires move through us as elusively as wind in trees.

When we feel our part in the dynamic motion of change, a fresh kind of stillness keeps us centered in the upheaval. We know that this, too, shall pass.

Like Wind in Trees

Zen mind cherishes uncertainty.
Stop struggling and give yourself to
it. Trust your inner sight and let
things come and go as they will.

Risk Everything

Go ahead, see things as they are,
not as you desire them to be, and
let the answers come on their
own terms.

Lean on nothingness:
It will support you.

Movement

Movement is the only law of the
universe. Sometimes after planting
a garden and watching it bloom,
there is no choice but to leave
it behind.

Everything Passes

"Everything passes" is a likely Zen
motto. The transitory nature of
worldly things adds perspective.
When life serves up a bitter pill, we
can more easily surrender things
we've already outgrown.

101

Shell Game

Making yourself happy? Can't be
done. Letting yourself become
happy? Easier than changing a hat.

Life Force, Life Surrender

Call it God, call it crocus, call it standing in line at the market. No matter what you say, it stays the same, in everything, always.

One River, Endless Streams

If you open yourself to the moment, you are at one with the moment. If you open yourself to life, you are at one with life. And its abundance pours in.

Forgiveness

Ignorance of the moment leaves
the heart frozen in the past.

Different Idea, Same Response, Part Two

Solitude, poverty, rigor: Be a
monk and have them if you want.
Comfort, fame, riches: Fine, go
ahead and have them too. With or
without, Zen mind is content with
a sunset and a thimbleful of tea.

Quick! No hurry at all.

Rooted in the Real

Leave behind all practices, all
scripture, all grasping. Face your
life free and stalwart as an elm.

Without Fail

The truly stable person changes
every day.

letting go

Holding on is a habit that we learn as children. The tighter we cling—to things, people, ideas, and all attachments—the smaller our world becomes. We're so afraid to yield anything that we end up forfeiting vital chances to grow.

The problem is that we identify with the things we've accumulated, internally and externally. We think we're only as good as the objects we own. Or only as real as our job, self-image, or belief system.

Eventually, our personal inventory becomes a burden that grows heavier over time. The older we get, the harder it is to just let go.

There's a Zen trick to ending this

syndrome. It begins with seeing that nothing really belongs to us—yet recognizing that we have *everything*. All we lack is the knowledge that real life doesn't occur in possessing and controlling things: It arises from a deep sense of belonging in the world and in the cosmos.

One Pure Taste

The life force that pervades
everything cannot be defined or
held onto. Enjoy it like a
mouthful of rain.

Having by Letting Go

Trying always to understand something, we miss everything. Trying always to hold something, we lose everything. What *is* everything? The ever-changing moment that we constantly lose—but can always find again.

Avoid life. It finds you anyway.

117

Find without Seeking

What do you see in other people?
Do you see *them,* or your desires
and expectations? Chasing things
pushes satisfaction out of reach.
Clinging to people leaves you
empty-handed. Let things be and
you will see what is real.

No Such Thing as Tomorrow

Nothing can be done about tomorrow. You cannot even grasp the next second from now in your hands. Even this moment slips away as soon as it arrives.

Ecstatic Emptiness

Pay attention, hold nothing, have
everything at once.

Back to the Present

To awaken a student from mental
slumber, a Zen master will strike
the floor with a *keisaku* ("encour-
agement stick"). The snapping
sound cuts off the past and delivers
the student back home to the
moment.

Choosing a Master,
Part One

Serve life, not ideas.
Serve love, not its image.
Serve the moment, nothing else.

Empty Hands, Open Mind

Nothing to hold onto, nothing to
own. This is the simple truth of
the present. All else is a phantasm,
gone before it appears.

Letting It Be

Force nothing. Then observe how
much energy you'll have to spare.

Honest Conduct

Express your real nature as it is.
Act well, care not for reward. Act
badly, care not for reproach.

Everywhere and Nowhere

Truth cannot be contained in any
one idea, but lives in every vessel
of existence.

Everywhere and Nowhere, Just More

Life is not limited to the limited way we receive it. It is expressed in endless forms, on endless occasions. Looking too hard, you miss the moment of truth.

Always Right, Anyway

Whatever you think about a thing—
it is different from that!

Spiritual Life, Part One

Spiritual life is the art form of appreciating things as they are, rather than as we wish them to be. When ordinary life starts to feel richer than your fantasies, simplicity in the soul will flow naturally as a mountain stream.

Let the World Reign Itself

When we interfere with the flow of
life, the balance crumbles. When
we approach each person with surrender, we fortify the whole. This
letting go is real inner security.

Work like playing, play like working.

131

Useless Words

Life cannot be described.
Better to say nothing at all.

Choosing a Master, Part Two

Information is fine, but transformation is the point. The two rarely converge.

The Ghost of Control

We try to control life because we think it will establish an order we desire. But control does not create order: Conversely, it generates tension and chaos. Let go and let life arrange itself naturally, without contrivance.

Spiritual Life, Part Two

Practicing Zen is merely attending to everything around you. Pay attention to how carefully you pour the tea, without spilling any. Or spill a drop of tea and notice you have done it.

Fixing things? What a shame!

Choosing a Master,
Part Three

Self looks on and watches the mind
scatter the soul . . . till it finally
tires of cleaning up the mess.

living compassion

The merciful heart is not a hazy, romantic idea. It is a highly practical state of being in response to distinct realities that affect every one of us. Without compassion, there can be no meaningful way to address the suffering that is part of human existence on Earth.

Each of us is here for only a brief moment in time. None of us escapes that fate. Zen mind understands that our mutual vulnerability is actually our most common strength. If we each receive one another as a living part of ourselves, we dissolve the illusion that any one person is better than the next. This is the humbling force that naturally produces kindness and respect.

Authentic compassion for others automatically includes oneself. We must first accept our own fragility and imperfection and let this acceptance reveal the depth of our connection to other people. When we see ourselves as one, we bless every living thing.

Wherever

An office or a mountaintop:
Wherever you sit, open your heart
to the world.

Ready for Seed

Humble as a soil bed: This is the
path to love.

There Already

We are nearer to truth than our
own heartbeats.

One Song

The sages speak in a hundred
different tongues, but their
meaning is one.

Open Your Eyes

There is nothing that is not a sign
of oneness.

Balance and Benevolence

Unconditional love is an offering
that keeps the world from going off
its axis. It's a reminder of what we
are all born to become.

How can you elude compassion?
It knows you already.

No Boundaries

Treasuring the moment empowers
you to emit compassion into the
world. When love extends beyond
the boundaries of your own four
walls, it serves all of life.

Quiet Treasure

Zen is best expressed in "small" things, in simple kindness toward others, no matter what the circumstances. Everything in life is interconnected and every positive action, however small it may be, helps to nourish the world.

Open Ears

Listen in a crowd as if you are
alone. Listen to another, as your
attention will keep him awake.
Listen like an ox walking to the
river. Leave argument in the trash
can where it belongs.

On Your Own, Part Two

No one outside yourself can give
you anything of value. Be alive to
yourself in all your joys and grief.
Harsh reality is a window to sweet
liberation.

Wherever You Are

All the teachings of Zen gather in a
thin slip of sunlight on your wrist.

Learning to Learn

Knowing nothing, how can we
reject anything?

This poor Earth, alone in her bed.

Homespun

Nothing real stays tidy for very long. We are knit into the cloth of life, like a burr woven into rough country wool.

Owning the Present

Even in a state of crisis, everything
is perfect. We make it so by adjust-
ing to things as they are, then
uplifting the circumstances with
compassion.

Nothing Else but This

Real compassion moves as naturally
as blood flows into the heart.

Home Remedy

The world is its own cure: By
loving, you become the hands that
deliver the medicine.